bound(less)

A Chandra

BookLeaf
Publishing

India | USA | UK

Presentation by *BookLeaf Publishing*

Web: www.bookleafpub.com

E-mail: info@bookleafpub.com

ISBN : 9789357449014

First edition 2021

Blank Page

Thoughts of everything
yet nothing
mix and meld
inside the empty chamber
of my head.

Why is it so hard to say what I mean?
To have the words flow out of me,
at double the speed.

But what if I have nothing to say?
No thought that deserves the moment of day.
Who wants to hear from
a girl,
a child,

a nothing.

What more could you add to the world,
When silence is but preferred?

Can't Take What You Give

I don't answer your calls.
Yet, I expect you to answer mine.

I don't reply to your texts,
Yet, I expect you to reply to mine.

Life isn't a one-way street,
now that is definitely true.
Then why do I make our relationship,
never according to you?

Click, Clack

Click.
An empty gallery staring back at me.
No faces to the names I've gotten used to see.
How do we connect from miles apart?
Is this really a replacement for physical touch?

Sit in silence for the day,
make one or two comments for display.
Stare blankly out the window for a while.
Rest my eyes from the screen time they have
compiled.

Clack.
That's me "signing off".
The daily tasks make it hard to stay aloft.
Despite the day nearing its end,
my thoughts continue to extend.

Returning to the room that was never gone.
The virtual world now withdrawn.
Take three steps to the bed,
to repeat the monotony in the days ahead.

Comfort

I stand in the kitchen,
staring out the window.
Listening to the rumble,
that is slowly starting to grow.

Pushed the switch a thousand times,
know the crescendo coming to life.
Wait for the click, and silence to follow.
Fill my cup to relieve the strife.

Take a seat in the sun.
Slowly sip as thoughts collect,
tranquillity forms in my head.
This is my ritual to reflect.

Defensive Play

You waltzed into the picture
and were nice enough at first.
Nothing too alarming,
that would mean we couldn't converse.

Then cracks started to appear.
Why? I do not know.
I lost interest, retreated.
Widening the chasm starting to grow.

Was it the way your other relationships
blossomed,
whilst ours lay untended to?
Or was it those small idiosyncrasies,
that finally began to accrue.

Once the damage was done,
our fate was sealed.
My prejudices overtook me,
leaving your actions unconcealed.

You did nothing wrong.
It was actually me at fault.
Too scared? stupid? insecure? to let you in.

Leaving me alone, by default.

6

Distant

Breathing the same air,
propinquity of space
yet remoteness of mind.

The words feel unnatural,
strangely forced.
Every encounter leaves me unaffable.

It takes one of us to extend a branch,
I think you tried,
but my tongue whiplashed.

Is it my ego? my pride?
My snap to judgement,
leaving both of us confined.

Is it too late to turn it around?
First, my humility needs to be roused.

Do Better

Angelic to an untrained eye,
"she's nice enough", they said.
But they don't know her other side,
and when it writhes its head.

Cold and calculating,
It's the side you don't want to see.
When she disapproves of you,
there is no salvation to foresee.

Selfish and proud,
the world according to her.
Don't get in the midst of it,
or you will get burnt.

Jealous and insecure,
the hurt stems from within.
Forms a cold exterior,
to never let anyone in.

Hurt people hurt people,
is that what they say?
Take control and stop the cycle,
make tomorrow a better day.

Dwell

Every conversation,
imprints on my imagination.
Etched in stone,
to revisit in another situation.

The good and the bad.
The happy and the sad.
I hold no agency,
over the ones forbad.

Unexpected visitors, uninvited guests.
Serial overthinker, makes me feel like a mess.

Failure

Failure.
What is so scary about it?
Doesn't it mean that you couldn't reach what
you wanted,
but not that you have absconded.

Trying again isn't a sin.
A hit to the ego that's paper-thin.
But it's nothing too cruel,
giving you space to take stock and refuel.

Truly unavoidable, one of life's certainties.
Then trying to avoid it is surely an absurdity.
Attempting to use all the might you can muster,
will only make it hit you harder and knock out
some bluster.

How to deal with it then when it comes along?
Let it push you to work harder,
and prove them all wrong.

Go For It

When an opportunity presents,
you go for it, right?
Push away those insecurities,
that make you feel like taking flight.

Thoughts start to spiral,
you can't have tricked everyone, right?
Into giving you a chance that,
looks so bright.

There are two roads to take.
You can't pass this up, right?
So lean into the discomfort,
and work to soar to new heights.

Is One the Loneliest Number?

Alone in a sea of people.
All connections are merely feeble.

A bystander, watching the world pass.
Floating through the crowd with no mass.

Hearing the laughs from around.
But barely there to make a sound.

Soon forgotten, leaving no mark.
Slowly sink back into the dark.

Despite others littering the scene.
Lonelier, I've never been.

Lassitude

The piercing shriek begins to grow.
Fumbling hands move haphazardly,
to silence the oncoming roar.
Yet the sound can't shake awake,
the hopes of the previous day.

"Early bird catches the worm",
but do you even want it?
Living life for the future you,
can slowly lose its purpose.

What is the goal of the grind?
For fame? fortune and power?
Are these things you ever wanted,
so why let them keep you devoured?

Happiness is all one can ask for,
but what does that even mean?
In an endless game where more isn't good
enough,
what is the point of this routine?

Mileage

Aching legs
Pounding head.
How far to push? My body pled.

Shaky steps.
Heavy breath.
Time to summon my inner strength.

They say it's mind over matter, but is this what
they mean?
Is pulsating pain how it's supposed to feel?

Look into the distance
Run to the post.
Trick my mind into thinking that we're getting
close.

Where is this high that I'm supposed to feel?
Like a dog chasing its tail,
it seems endless to me.

One foot in front of the other.
Take a gulp of fresh air.
Embrace the feeling of being weightless through
the air.

Prisoner

Caught in a steel trap.
The external world living in a different reality,
to my internal confines.

Isolation is not good for the soul.
Time spent thinking alone,
widens the chasm starting to grow.

Have I been forgotten by the outside world?
It seems that the laughter just continues,
with no call for tissues.

Escape is allowed,
just not possible.
A self-imposed prison,
with only me to reverse the decision

Selfless

Your example was the holy grail.
Teaching right from wrong, hoping good would prevail.

Your presence exudes sunshine in a room,
providing people with the elements to bloom.

Seemingly endless love you have to give,
always ready to forgive.

A stronger moral compass I have never seen,
doing the right thing has become a routine.

"Kindness will make you strong",
making others feel like they belong.

Though those around you tend to excel,
please make sure to leave some love for you as well.

The Lake

Under the tunnel,
up the path.
Watching children ride their bikes,
as if they were adults.

Pass some runners
and some walkers.
Polite nods and smiles,
as we brush shoulders.

Take a step off the path.
beeline to left,
for the mound of grass.

Take a seat on the hill.
Shrouded by the bushes,
It feels oh so still.

Stare out, onto the lake.
So peaceful are its waters,
it makes life feel like no mistake.

Two Halves

The rich and the poor.
The protector and the saboteur.

The lucky and the unfortunate,
The senior and the subordinate.

We live in a world divided,
but does one side have to win?

Is life a zero-sum game,
or are we all just living in sin?

Seeing across the gaps,
now that is something we lack.

To put away the biases,
and just see people for what their true desire is.

What Will Everyone Think?

Sweaty palms, parched throat.
Breathing through the panic,
that is swiftly being evoked.

Soon my time on the stage.
All eyes turn to see,
what I can say to keep them engaged.

Starting slow, senses heightened,
Petrified of slipping up,
given away by eyes widened.

Then it begins to fade into a blur.
Picking up momentum,
oblivious to any stir.

Sprinting my way to the end.
A sigh of relief,
this time I won't be condemned.

But does any of it really matter?

Isn't everyone too wrapped up in their own world,
for it to ever cause much chatter.

Who Am I?

Innocent question,
Makes you feel like you don't belong.
Always being in the minority,
Makes you feel like there is something wrong.

Distancing yourself from who you really are.
Relinquishing your identity,
just to try and join the club.

The world is a tough place to go it alone.
Strength in numbers,
throughout the hurdles it throws.

Trying to fit in isn't a crime.
But must it come at the cost,
of forgetting who you are on the inside?

You

You were the one who tucked me in at night,
the one who made me laugh.
You were the one who read me bedtime stories,
until we both collapsed.

You were the one who taught me to ride a bike,
the one who would catch my fall.
You were the one who showed me new places,
before I grew frail and old.

You were the one who hurt me deeply,
through your tempers and rage.
You were the one whose moods would swing
making life a balancing game.

You were the one who would say you're sorry,
getting me to forgive.
You were the one to do it all again,
making me feel like a kid

You were the one who never seemed to
understand,
the power that you held.
You were the one who shaped me, scraped me
taking away the love I had to give.

You were the one who said you wanted the best
for me,
but it seems like you just wanted the best for you
instead.

Zeroth Minute

Do I, or don't I?

Putting something out there for the world
is never something I undertook frivolously.
Edit upon edit, correction upon correction,
Barely ready to showcase it until it was reaching
perfection.

The world can be judgemental, that is for sure.
But if I can survive my inner voices then my
work is secure.
Never sharing is the safe way to go.
But how do I learn, grow,
and leave any permanence beyond my ego?